rooted
and
winged

megan dire

for: b, bird, and buggy
may your dreams always be
bigger than your fears!

a seed is where
this story starts,
full of promise,
full of heart

she dreamed
of growing
strong and tall,
it seemed
impossible for
she was so small

4

but from her seed a root breaks through, anchored to the soil and then: she grew

5

what started as one
became many more,
and soon she was
taller than she
was before

once a seed,
now a sprout,
above the soil
she looks about

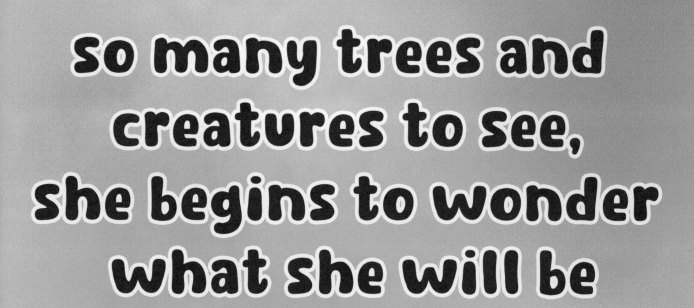

so many trees and
creatures to see,
she begins to wonder
what she will be

the sun gives way
and clouds roll in,
she senses a storm
is about to begin

as rain comes down,
she is filled with fear,
overwhelmed with
doubt, her future
is unclear

but when thunder
crashed and wind
howled along,
she stayed rooted
in what made
her strong

then through those roots, her leaves grew like wings, and now she is grateful for the spring

every storm brought
a lesson, one she
would need,
to fulfill her
purpose, to become
THIS tree

her journey
encourages and her
branches are home,
she reminds others
that they are not
alone

and from the
top it's all so clear,
the world needed
the story that
grew her here

Made in United States
Troutdale, OR
12/12/2023

15761367R00019